MW01115179

Prose from many shores

—⟨∞⟩——

Heaven's Echo

BUD SIMMONS

ISBN 978-1-63903-218-1 (paperback)
ISBN 978-1-63903-219-8 (digital)

Copyright © 2022 by Bud Simmons

All rights reserved. No part of this publication may be reproduced, distributed, or transmitted in any form or by any means, including photocopying, recording, or other electronic or mechanical methods without the prior written permission of the publisher. For permission requests, solicit the publisher via the address below.

Christian Faith Publishing
832 Park Avenue
Meadville, PA 16335
www.christianfaithpublishing.com

Printed in the United States of America

To Mark Walkingstick, who was and remains
a loyal dedicated friend and mentor.

"come away my beloved and be like the gazelle or like
a young stag on the spice laden mountains."

—song of songs 8:6

Contents

Preface

So many years ago, I read my first poem "The Ballad of William Sycamore" by *Steven Vincent Benet* from whence a fire began inside me to chase words and connect them to what I saw and felt. I began carrying a spiral notebook and BIC pen, scribbling down what I observed in life.

A profound awareness came over me. The magic of life itself could be transformed into words that could feed the soul. The presence of the muse was one that dazed me at first as I found myself writing at the end or beginning of each day.

I researched my curiosity and came up with many answers or suggestions—God speaking to us, souls who ask their stories to be told, the Divine awareness that you are not alone when writing—and these are not your words.

Writing of my own experience of encounters (there are no chance encounters) for when we meet another person is meant to be.

Here in this unique collection, you will find much devoted to the Divine and psalms that came to me during early morning prayers or, as I titled this book, Prose from many shores: Heaven's Echo.

In this lyrical expression of love, loss, war, and early morning visits by the muse (heaven's echo), it is my fervent hope and prayer that reading these words will inspire and encourage the reader's awareness that it is never too late to pursue your dreams in whatever category you have chosen.

Remember to invite God into all your endeavors and that prayer and love remain the strongest force in the Universe, for he created us with worthiness and value.

Wishing you love and light on your reading of *Prose from many shores: Heaven's Echo.*

Acknowledgments

I wish to thank Mark Walkingstick, who was and remains a loyal and dedicated friend and mentor. I would also like to thank Dr. Leslie Worthington.

Also, thanks to Derek Disney, Bill Hall, Peggy Morris, and John Bartlow.

Thank you to the members of my Thursday evening writers' group as follows: Douglas Polk, Karen Greco, and Patty Williams.

Special thanks Christian Faith Publishing and my Publication Specalist, Karen Franz, for all that they do.

Without all of the above people this book never would have been written.

To those wonderful otherworldly whispers of heaven's echo that led to the title of this book and to its now publication.

Introduction

I am drawn to writing every morning as though a fish to water. The muse whispers to me from many guises and genres many times. It's like some otherworldly voices are dictating the story of what you will read on these pages.

Herein are many stories. Most are Christian based. Many are psalm-like poetry, and others include history stories of someone's life struggles, loss, growth, the road to recovery and change, salvation, and redemption.

Within these pages are essays written in stanzas from the muse, who is always present during my prayer and meditation time; hence, the words come.

It is my hope you will be inspired by the reading *Prose from many shores: Heaven's Echo* and pursue your own dreams in life to the fullest.

Introduction

Prose from many shores: Heaven's Echo

Herein is an assortment of inspirational writings and words of encouragement. It is a mixture of spiritual poetry and stories. Some are modern-day psalms that came to me during prayer and meditation. It is meant to inspire tired souls and encourage those of us who desire to follow our dreams.

Also, it is meant to hopefully broaden the scope of establishing a closer relationship with God as you understand God.

Sometimes, the road to heaven takes many twists and turns; as the author of this book, my life began in St. Louis in August of 1942—the mists of World War II.

Being raised by a single working mom and grandmother and an only child, life was a struggle, to say the least. I do not want to bore you, dear reader, with the ups and downs of a challenging childhood, so I will be brief here. I was raised by great aunts and a grandmother. I left school at fourteen and pursued a life of drugs and alcohol.

I found recovery and Jesus Christ. I am clean and sober now for forty-four years. I owe it all to God.

Hopefully, you will find some tools that may be helpful to you within these pages. And whatever you may find and/or discover, they are, at times I feel, from a heavenly source as the muse presented them, which is why I titled this work *Prose from many shores: Heaven's Echo*.

Bud Simmons, Houston, Texas, 2021

Poetry

Noun. The art of rhythmical composition, written
or spoken, for exciting pleasure by beautiful,
imaginative, or elevated thoughts.

A Horse Named Destiny (1836)

A quiet corpse-like breeze chases dried magnolias
Across the plains as I watch another Texas sunset
There is an ambiance that calls me to something
I'm not certain of.

As in my past dreams, a white mare awaits me
I climb upon the polished leather saddle and
Again, the déjà vu permeates every fiber of my being
As she swings into full gallop into the vortex of
scores of my dreams and visions.

I'm distracted by the sound of flapping
Looking over my shoulder the March wind ignites
The snapping of a flag, red, white, and green with
1824 emblazoned in the center.

Men in buckskin with Kentucky rifles walk about
With half-grown boys, a friendly dog follows them
I see oxen and women, a few toddlers, a Tejano boy
Lays a tin down for a friendly, hungry cat.

Two Negro men with pick and shovel dig a well
I see them although they see me not. It dawns
Now with inner being this mare I am on is the one
They call Destiny.
I have returned. I am at long last home.
Atgofion

The first customer this autumn morning
The large Latino waitress pours me a cup
Caffeine.

A young Tejano lad opens the blinds, the
Texas sunrays sneak their rays across the floor.

My early morning still foggy mind unravels
In movie projector fashion memories.

That torture me in my dreams. The ghost of a gray
Cat (that only I can see) purrs in my ear.

As magnificent a life you live now in
An otherworldly paradise.

A profoundness grips my being as I
Think of you I intuitively know at this exact
Given moment in time you are thinking of me.

Memories of a Republic

A cadaverous wind entices dancing tumbleweeds
Across this hallowed ground, I trudge
The sense of being gripped by a ghostly presence
Permeates me within.

Bleached bones of horse and warrior alike
Give a vivid glow against the harvest moon
Rusted swords and broken muskets
Weather beaten and broken stand in silent vigil.

The whistle of nature's shifting sounds
Hammers at my still unanswered question
What brings me to such a hauntingly possessing
Place, Eden could not have been this alluring.

On a distant Texas wind, a corpse-like presence
Beckons from a world I whiff a vague remembrance of
A red and white sky emerges from a coming dawn
That whispers to me yet again
I am denied my world from whence I crave.

Broken Hallelujah

Word had it he came from the open plains of Texas
Traveled north in 1870 buckskin and coonskin cap
Made his home with the Cheyenne and the Sioux
Fell in love with a maiden name of *Running Brook*

So such the legend goes, then he left his people
Of the plains signed on with the US Army under
Son of the Morning Star, Custer.

The maiden herself by this time loved *Crazy Horse*
Honored this day to ride by his side in the battle against
The now-dreaded Custer and his Horse Soldiers.

Ride not sir into the valley of the big horn river
He pleaded. Thinking of his *Running Brook*
For the Sioux and Cheyenne are angry.

"We will ride, and you with us" came a condescending reply.
Anger was our greatest weapon that day she would
Say many times around many counsel fires in the
Decades that followed.

Custer died with his ego that day along with five companies
Of United States Cavalry—it was the beginning of the end
To a great plains people and horse culture.

She of course could but wonder of her first love
And why he never returned to her or the people
He said he loved so dearly.

Do I now but walk this hallowed ground
As again a sense of déjà vu grips me of
Warrior braves along with soldiers who
Died that day.

As whispers of corpse-like
Voices remind me of unwritten poetry
And life stories so untold.

Butt-Scratchin' Encounter

I was on the veranda of that quick shop
And truck stopped just a tad west of Nacogdoches
Drinking a Royal Crown cola
Brown-faced workers and Latino ladies
Hurried about with chores washing, and
Buying lotto tickets
"Seems like you back here again," a voice behind me said.
Turning about I saw him, long tall cowboy-like fella
Stetson, boots the works
"We talked once before, didn't we?" he said.
"Yeah, when that oil truck come through here, talked bout
Dem dancing girls in New Orleans. Some are girls anyway, right?"
"You a writer, ain't cha?"
"Now I remember," I said. "You ask a bunch
of questions. You a damn cop or
Somethin'?"
"Ask me somethin', Mr. Writer."
"Youse a poet and don't know it—hee haaaaaa." He laughed.
"I member now. I know you from way back dare another time."
"You love Texas, yeah? I know ya."
A forty-nine ford came by, he got in it drove off.
I scratched my butt and woke up.

Echo of a Broken Covenant

The mournful cry of the coyote broke the
Silence under this clear night of an infinity
Of endless stars.

The brisk winds of March numbed his fingers
As he stood his watch from the wall he could
See the dying flames from Salado's campfires.

Surrounded now by brown-skinned men all
In battle order who have sworn for you and
Your brethren there will be *no quarter*
So where now was the fortune and fame that so
Lured him to this Texas plain.

And would his parents ever know of his death
For now, it had been made certain, the snap and
Crack of the flag in the wind gave little comfort now
With the opening of Salado's cannonade.

In now he mustered defiance and yelled a warning
Of an onslaught of waves of green, red, and white banners
Along with thousands of Salado's possessed-like screaming men
Now in his mind, he could but hope—
History would be kind.

El Degüello Rising

The band played its relentless notes
That this morning's strong breeze
Carried a most haunting sound over the mission walls.
The sound echoed and reverberated its
Message to already-exhausted men that
Their next reality was to be eternity.

Tejano children huddled in the chapel
Taking comfort from a furry cat, the
Ghostly music and trumpets affected them not.
Soon the cannonade would drown out the
Music that signaled the *no quarter*
And soon possessed-like *soldado* men
Would charge the walls, with axes and scaling ladders.

As he stood on the wall he watched as Travis
Bid the last courier a safe gallop, a final plea
For aid to a not-yet-new republic? Or perhaps
Because the courier was sixteen?

The increased March winds
Brought a snapping sound
To the flag of 1824 that waved
From the walls.

Tennessee Echo

For thirteen long days now, he had thought
of his boyhood days in Tennessee
Catfish jumping and a squirrel gun
Upon which he cut his teeth.
The ambiance that surrounded him of
scents of the Tennessee wilderness
Of his grandpa's tales of fighting the British,
his father and he is chopping
firewood.
He stood his watch on the wall, knowing a
determined foe who had sworn
no quarter.
Was likely to overwhelm this old adobe
Spanish mission, converted to a
makeshift fortress.
An early march wind brought the smell
of wood-burning fires from the
enemy camp.

Gabriel's Call

With speed like not before he pushed his horse
Panting with rapid adrenaline it was as if even his
Steed sensed the urgency to tell the settlers and
Goliad what the archangel Gabriel bellowed.

"Can you hear him callin'? The Alamo has fallen."

This March day was chilled, the smell of magnolias
And the wildness of the Texas plain, along with the distant
Smoke of a funeral pyre.

The horse rearing on its hind legs, the buckskinned rider
Bellows fetch your oxen, and what food ya might need
Texas is in a bind, and they ain't far behind.

"Can't you hear Gabriel callin'? The Alamo has fallen."

Someone rides on to the Brazos won't you please, muster
Who you might, for alas a final fight
For only now one voice is callin'—My God, the Alamo has fallen.

"Tell Rosita, sir, if you see her. I was obligated to remain in Goliad."

Small Texas Town

I loved a small Texas town, where folks all
Socialized and know one another's name
And the locals all showed up for the
High school Friday night game
All before this thing called technology took us all over.

Can still recall grandpas grin when he'd mutter
"I wish Texas was Texas again."
Industrial monsters on the march covered the
Plain with strip malls, gas stations, convenience
Stores and overworked men.
In this twilight time of my days, I hear grandpa mutter
"I wish Texas was Texas again."

King of Kings

Underneath a Texas sky filled with still
A trillion winking stars my pony and me
Alone though we may be
Fear not the blackness or nocturnal
Sounds of coyotes, predators, and such
For in this vast vortex of our being I
Sense again the presence of the King of Kings.

Your words resonate within
Hear me, King of Kings, oh
So again, as thee did then
King of Kings, you're here with me
Here to see me through, King of Kings, I so love you.

Tears of joy from my weary eyes
Catch the glimpse of a new sunrise
King of Kings, ride with me now
No longer lost and so alone
King of Kings, you're guiding us home.

The Road to Nacogdoches

The road to Nacogdoches won't you tell me how it was
Was it rainy, muddy, or filled with frightened Texicans
Were you content with what you choose? and the sacred
door behind you closed.

A raven followed you that day, and some called you coward
Some begged for names of loved ones who stayed, you were
Told embraced them lovingly.
Your flop brown hat knapsack and moccasins and musket across
You're back the skin of a wild boar as a strap.

Tell me again, kind sir, of those grim-
faced men, who knew they were
To die, and why you choose not the oppressor's sword.
Simple life extended choice
Courier after courier Travis sent—No
volunteers came so over the wall
You went.

Might I say by the couriers that were sent
and Travis pleas ignored by
those
Who called themselves Texans
Might history now redirect its accusations at who the real cowards
May have been—yet enjoyed the later benefits of a free republic?

Price for a Republic

A corpse-like stillness driven by a March wind
Haunts this vast wilderness of dust and sand
The occasional sound of musketry finds yet
Another defender, refusing to admit
His expendability.

Smoke rises from a smoldering pyre
Filling the nostrils with the ugly stench
Of burning flesh in a shattered mission
That failed as a fortress.

Bleak images of crippled and tired oxen
Pull a wagon of weeping women and
A child, guided by two Negro men, as a soldado
Tries to offer verbal comfort.

Through the flames of the pyre is
Yet another blurred image that of
Another soldado picking up a long
Kentucky rifle examining it with dubious eyes.

Ride Like the Wind

Ride you now like never before
final word that you bring to the world
look not back again
ride you now like the wind.

Fill not your destiny yet to come
for you and your steed are now one
to choose life over death is no sin
ride you now lad like the wind.

Forget you never this bleak march night
nor the struggle or freedoms cries or
the look in Travis's eyes, or the tears in your own.

With the clap, snap of the flag in the wind
galloping hard and fast over hill and dale
soldados scattering out of your path
ride you now like never before
ride you now, lad, like the wind.

For James Allen, last known courier from the Alamo
March 5, 1836—Texas Ranger, Indian fighter, Civil War
soldier, Mayor of Indianola, Texas, died age eighty in 1901

William Travis (Revisited)

"Fashionable it is today," the history teacher said.
To bash these men of honor seeing their all dead
My colleagues and I would most certainly be wide-eyed
Should they reappear and remind us *Texas* is why they died.
In history, professors lounge at colleges and universities
They yet conjure images of buckskin cavaliers and men
Of masculine stature the fantasy of standing where they stood
The legacy still explodes into legends, stories, and a noble cause
Yet who knew you more than the age you
served, the trails you blazed
The battles you fought
Unshaven, unbathed months on end, whiskey in place of water
Rash, many times raciest slave owners
What might today's society rob you of? There are cries of
Striking your name from schools, roads, and buildings because
You owned a slave and lived a life today
that remains in the crosshairs
Of the *politically correct* (and those who dare to rewrite history)
Write what they may leave them with what they say
In the bleak images of my boyhood days, it was you who
Stood with honor, praise, and shine
William Travis, you are yet a hero of mine.

Ruby the Alamo Cat

Older generations in an earlier San Antonia spoke
Of otherworldly encounters more as merely passing
Conversations.
Alamo guards and staff talk of a far-flung feeling
While making rounds from time to time.
Recording frequently that *Ruby* the cat would act
In a strange manner strutting through the chapel as
If an unseen presence loomed near, sometimes very nearby.
What strange and unforeseen knowing's does our
Egos rob us of.
Might I see what Ruby sees—only if I were who Ruby is
My need and craving for this sacred shrine that haunts me
In my dreams.
Ruby, tell me who you see and what mysteries and truth
Do you hold?
I pour your water and vittles in a bowl and leave you to inter
Mingle with spirits of heroes I know but from my boyhood days
Ruby, 'tis you I envy.

Sacred Echo

A corpse-like stillness driven by a slow breeze
Haunts the empty plains of this prairie wilderness
I am caught in a seemingly vortex type of déjà vu
With a knowing of a faraway remembrance.
The aroma of sweat and leather permeates
My nostrils coupled with the roasting of wild
Pig over an open fire, linseed oil, and hunting
Tools sometimes clanging with bowie knives.
There is that smell of mules and horse dung
Men dressed in buckskin and knee-high moccasins
Lean on their long Kentucky rifles swapping stories
Of home and woodland adventures.
Men, mules, oxen, horses not to mention dogs
Lost now on the shoreline of a far-flung eternity
After giving all for a new republic, ah, do I not
Visit thee in my dreams.
This sacred cradle of my boyhood days of long ago
That the Texans still call the Alamo.

Son of 1941

Look for me not in your high school history books
hear my name neither from a lecture of
your university, professor, nor
scholars yet to come

I am a son of 1941
I cherished my country from the top of
rolling boxcars and an occasional
sympathetic truck driver, trading my labor
for two dollars and a meal, lost
soul to many, to others a bum
I am a son of 1941

From the soup lines of the cities to those
West Virginia coal mines, to
unheard of mountain streams and orchards

With no jobs and little hope, I traded in my dungarees for a military
uniform
three meals now every day and money in
my pocket, showers, and a bed
new friends to sing and run
hey, I am a son of 1941

Find me not on the heroes register, but I'll
be below you when you visit the
Arizona at Pearl Harbor. I rest in the silence
of the nights at Guadalcanal
and unmarked graves and caves of Bataan
and Corregidor and Singapore

Come let our souls be chums, we are the sons of 1941
might I now cradle in my arms the orphans of Hiroshima?
as a son of 1941

But in My Dreams

Can't we ever go back only in our dreams as precious moments
Become so ever more precious only when
they are gone, and you with
them.

Can I but see only now however dear you were to me
As I let the wonders of life and others take precedence
Only to finally come to grips with the realization you and you
Alone were my greatest gift.

I remember so much now in these twilight years
A country girl who made me a man.

Roving hills and distant song headlong into life
With all its ramblings and demands of maturity
Which cannot come without pain and suffering a
World that demanded accountability of which I
Had none.

I remember now being surrounded by love and
So many who loved me, tolerated me, and held
Me up, picked me up, never could I have gotten
Here without you.

Your love gave me strength when my
Okayness was contingent on an unforgiving world
When fear ruled every fiber of my being.

Childhood Days

Can I reflect on those childhood days
when Karen McCredie and I would
walk to school, and I would carry her books
and sometimes it would stand easy enough to see
home would be the safest place to be
now tell me about your childhood days
were they filled with pain
or were they filled with praise
did they set the pattern for our lives
with pompous priests and ugly lies
was there one, just one, adult anywhere
who heard our cries,
leaving my childhood days behind
happiness came the day I sing, when
I turned and gave them all the finger
and said, "Damn you all, and damn you
all again."

Daffodils

This poem is one that I find great beauty
in and a good deal of personal
relationship within the fact that daffodils
surrounded the hills by the lake.
And springtime was one of those special
seasons that seemed to create
new life in nature, and William Wordsworth
certainly expresses this in
many of his poems.
I think his expression of the daffodils must be the imploding of an
emotional experience that only nature
can bring about.
I think he, like so many poets, is captivated by all things relating to
nature. On more than one occasion, I have
been struck by the beauty of
nature and found it impossible to express
it to anyone save for my pen
and notebook.
Having lived in the mists of the wilderness
and basking in its beauty is one
experience no aspiring poet should miss.

The Beast of Battle

Damn the beast of battle
mine eyes are damp with tears as
revenge tugs at every fiber of my being.
Where are the bands that played
so gaily and filled our spirits with
patriotism and excitement of war?
As far as my vision carried me
the only view is one of grief and
chaos dead and dying horse and hero mangled.
The colors mangled and torn
I lift from the grip of its loyal
carrier, hesitating only long
enough to unbuckle my belt.
The saber and pistol drop to
my feet, with colors in hand
I limp back to my mount and saddle.
I sing, "Damn this beast of battle."

Dawn Dance

I lie alone in the king-sized bed as the flickering
candle puts a show of dancing shadows across the ceiling.
My cradle of slumber I now leave behind, filled with the
majestic visions of a world I held in kind.
The ghost of a gray cat walks across my chest.
My consciousness navigates me to
a window long since closed but was by far both mystical
and otherworldly.
Through it became our Eden.
My consciousness leaves the window. I drift slowly now
back to this present moment and the presence of dawn.
At dawn, we danced outside under the shadow of the stone eagles
who guarded our walkway. I pretend we are again moving slowly.
My hand in yours, my joy, my life, my God.
I had the world, our window to Eden, me. I tasted the juices
of artistic imagination. I held in my hand's paradise beyond
dreams, with the life I shared with an
artist whose only quest was her
love of life and her love for me.

Deferred Honor

If in some realm of unsung heroes I should sing
For a starter, I would sing of Edward Carter.
You have sung your heroes full of praise
From wars long past of bygone days.
Hope never faded in Edward Carter's soul as racism
Pounded you deeper into that hole.
You never gave up on your country
And claimed it until the end.
Men like me with bowed head
Ask why can't we start this over again.
Sorry for my countrymen
Who let you die with a broken heart while so
Many could have looked to you for a positive start.

Dixie Dew

Another day sparks the Georgia pines and skies
Skies of coming blue and dripping from the pines
And flowers are early morning Dixie dew
I sing now of beauty I have known, wild birds, and
Living things that grew
Peace I find in nature's kind and alas the scent of
Early morning Dixie dew
Light-blue skies and gentle breeze put my mind at ease
My Atlanta home, nothing rings so true as that early
Morning Dixie dew

Doctor's Visit

Faces of the elderly with walkers
and middle-aged overweight men
with expressions of nervous anticipation.
People fill the waiting area while
nurses appear with clipboards
calling names and smiling the
receptionist chews gum and
reads insurance cards.
Stomachs growl from the directive
nothing after midnight that precedes
all lab works.
Empty eyes stare at the TV which is
always stuck on the DYI channel a
few nervously page through six months
old magazines.
I look at the TV and remember the
Gold Dust Twins from the 1950s.
A cleaning commercial.
It was racist.

Don't Kill the Swan

There is a Zen saying I learned years ago
Of a man who raised a baby swan in a glass jar.
The baby swan grew and became caught in the glass jar.
But it was the man who was now caught
For the only way to free the swan
Was to break the jar, killing the thing.
I can walk this path as many have done
Before me, I am at liberty to enjoy the
Fragrance of nature and beauty walk
Slowly this path of water, trees, and
Birds of such elegance and color.
How many swans have I killed by
Attempting to keep their beauty
To myself? A swan is a swan and must
Always remain beholding to the eye.
She must go her way in elegance
And grace, and the sight of her exquisiteness
Lingers within as another poet stated,
"Beauty seen is never lost."

Embarrassing Echo

It was lights out now and the bugler sounded taps
The hauntingly beautiful tone floated across the
Parade ground, the officer's quarters, motor pool, and
Cavalry stables.
The bugle seemed to be the motivating tool that
Everyone on an army base lived by, the sound of the
Bugler's call indicated the rising of the post colors the
Lowering, when chow was served when it was time
To rise in the morning and sleep time.
He had competed for *post bugler*. He was chosen
Over a Black soldier from the tenth cavalry the 1939 army
Was still segregated. He knew he was chosen because
He was White, the buffalo soldier was Black.
The buffalo soldier was immaculately dressed polished
And sharp, and he was a better bugler. He was better in
Every area of expertise. He could not help but feel
a sense of emptiness and despair.
Not that he would ever show it
That was something soldiers do not do.
Deep inside, he knew he was awarded the position of post bugler
Simply because he was White.

Enduring Wind

Young adults tedious of history
Dance above the ground that holds our
Bleached white broken bones and skulls
Where now half-a-century-plus men of
Different races clashed in the name of
National honor.
Tourists hurry on, haggling with merchants
Marble monuments to commemorate us
Now are cracked and sorrowfully scathed.
We were the generation of the 1930s
The men of *the grapes of wrath* who were
Born out of John Steinbeck's pen.
Our bones lie buried in the dirt and sand
In forever unmarked graves. What is left here to sow
but on moonlit nights, we dance to a now-forgotten echo.

But for the Memory of Essie

Her ancestry could easily have been traced
To an African warrior nation, she was tall and
Lanky smiling but on rare occasions, stern and
Tall in her starched white uniform.
She possessed the high cheekbones of
The Zulu people, and I could see her
In my mind's eye, dispatching British
Soldiers at Isandlwana or Rorke's Drift.
She made no secret of her contempt toward
Up to do Whites, and those of her own race
And culture she called *Uncle Toms* quick to
Anger yet slow to forgive, if indeed she ever did.
In her presence, I learned respect and compassion
As she related her life's experiences of oppression
Racism and struggling still for recognition and equality.
We learned quick to do as she directed
Reflecting now with hopeful thoughts her
Children and grandchildren found peace and acceptance
she herself was denied.

Camelot Echo (1960)

I hear those who talk of twilight years and
Fortunate enough to nurture memories along
With a few tears
What may or may not be the truth yet for me,
But I cherish a farmhouse by a crossroads that
Amazingly the progress of development passed by.
The promise of completeness now, as peace seemed
To engulf the land, roving hills, and hills, never-ending
Trees, acres without fences, your mom doing chores.
Your grandma frying chicken.
What an ambiance in the air, puberty gave way to adolescence
My head upon your breast, walking the dusty road your hand in
Mine, a time of magic never again to be duplicated.
For had there been a way, rest assured, I would have found it.
Was not life perfect, distant echoes of then call me in the dead
Of night, come back, come back to what was Camelot.
Why might I scream, could we not have kept it that way.
In the canyons of my yesterdays, you beckon yet to me from
That shoreline of Camelot.

Closing of the Door

I lie with closed eyes on my side wide awake
As you pack the last of your belongings, our
Goodbyes are done as dawn breaks, and you
Go quietly toward the door.
There are a hundred words I want to say, and
Yet I lie quiet as loneliness engulfs me, the
Ambiance of your scent of which I no more
Will know, as you move quietly toward the door.
When you go, I'll phone a friend who will tell me
Acceptance is the answer to all my problems
As he did a hundred times before.
And now you
Move quietly toward the door.
Images of us in happier times, like a videotape
Pass across my mind's eye, tortured by unspoken
Words, coldness in my stomach
that cries to my core
All with the gentle, closing of the door.

Clydesdales in the Snow

When slumber time approaches with the
Closing of each day, I close my eyes and
Lay me down, where you used to lay.
In a distant vision of a world where angels play
With an ambiance of light and aliveness like
I never knew.
Under a melting sky of buttermilk and blue
You're running with ghost Clydesdales, and long-haired
Hounds, where spirit knows no bounds.
There's a voice that calls from the canyon of
My yesterdays that just won't let me be
Twilight time is when you return to me, in
Your splendor and your charm
That invisible world where souls meet up again
And failed loves again begin to grow, I see you
Feeding sugar cubes to Clydesdales in the snow.
Wish I knew then now what I now know
Dreaming I'm there with you, playing with those
Clydesdales in the snow.

Boss Cat (Revisited)

He was as big as a man, at least six feet tall, big and furry
And stood on his hind legs, a black derby on his head
Bubblegum in his mouth, and a walking stick in his left paw
He danced to a Michael Jackson song. I locked my arm in his
As he said hey, "I'm Boss cat, and that's that." We started a
Dance down Peachtree Lane
Children and venders from everywhere they came
"Giving us room," a voice laughed out
"I know you ain't bride and groom"
On down the middle of the highway now
Workers joining in our dance
Traffic pulling over folks leaving their cars
Starting to dance with one another
MJ's voice blaring out. "You, my brother,
Don't matter if you're Black or White"
Boss cat and me doing double backflips
Cops lined up doing the *Cuban shuffle*
High fives and hugs everywhere
Me and Boss cat tap dancing quick
Now slow, side by side, side to side
Up then down, turning fast and
A double high fiving whoever close by
Boss cat backing away
ME: Where are you going, Boss cat?
BOSS CAT: It's time.
ME: You for real?
BOSS CAT: You know me—
ME: No, dude. No, I don't I just know. I love you
BOSS CAT: You should, I'm every cat and every dog
you ever loved
ME: Damn, Boss cat, wait a second, I
"The family's big orange-and-white cat
Bits walked across my chest as I woke up
"It's a Beautiful World" was playing on the radio.

Brave Echo

Might I say I have loved, and I was well in
Need of my own alms of forgiveness and
Giving, and by any stretch of imagination might
I say I was brave enough to love an equality
Brave and wild woman.
Who I shared sunsets and starry nights
Campfires and the most intimate moments
Of touching and laughter with, and never submitted
To society's expectations of womanhood.
That which enriches the soul and fires the psyche
More precious than riches of the world, I have found
Matches not loving a wild independent woman,
Was that my courage that nearly eluded me?
I stand now with no regrets, never again on a
Shoreline of uncertainty or dodging any omen
Grateful am I who dared to love a wild untamed woman.

Echo of Lost Love

Did the face of young Victoria truly captivate?
The hearts of a thousand royal guardsmen?
And Helen of Troy, whose face was said to
Launch a thousand ships, your face brought
To me new levels of a mystic delight.
When you smiled you gave joy to my physic
That made the summer breeze sweep through yet
Every fiber of my being (even though
winter winds outside blew hard)
Even now, sometimes between the sacredness of night
And the coming of the dawn
The deepened canyon of my yesterday's takes sway
To the ambiance of you.
The misty visions of my used-to-bes give me pause
To understand from deep inside why women ruled kingdoms
And created civilizations, while men choose war.

Fleeting Remembrances

The early morning mist of my yesterdays
Brings a remembrance of my used-to-bes
The smell of wildness from the Bayou as
Nocturnal critters make their way to yet
Unevaded habitats.
Two herons scold me in words I can't understand
Gliding low over an undisturbed lagoon, all of which
Brings to me the sweet ambiance of you, and the
Overall autumn of the dreams we so shared
The buck on the hill stands strong and proud
His attention radiates to unseen doe's waiting
In the wood
The sweet remembrance that takes me
Back to thee
The gentle purring of a ghost of a gray cat
Reminds me again, cherish the moment
For all we are, all we possess, all we love, is
Fleeting, ever fleeting.

Flowing Destiny

In the coolness of the evening
Breeze, I sense your presence
My yesterdays are filled with lingering
Aliveness and beauty of yet a time of
Carefreeness and abounding youth
Of fenceless hills that ran for miles
Of hikes in the hills and leaping
Over mountain streams and exploring
Uncharted caves
My yesterdays now feel like they may
Be forever gone lost now in the vast
Uncertainty of a thousand eternities
Shrouded in a hundred universes
But who among us can recalibrate
Destiny, sweet destiny who none
Escape and few fulfill,
Somewhere in a distant millennium
You wait, you wait again as you did then
And the red-tailed hawk has found me.

For Allen

Ah, what is it—this mystery of life and what does she hold?
But me and you what amounts in heaven's time to but a
Brief blink of the eye.
Can I but see now that life may have been kinder to you
With the roads you trudged and the sacrifices given
Made that most mothers make, yet go so unsung.
What might I perhaps thank you for higher than my birth
Bringing me into a world that even then you ask yourself
The dubious question of security and safety—yet choose
To give a soul life in our world, regardless.
I shall see your face in every sunrise and sunset
I will look upon your love and selflessness again
With every butterfly that lights nearby
The singing of every songbird, every joy I sense
I will know again, without you, this could never have been.
I will hear you again with every note I play and song I sing
And rest at last knowing you now live majestically in the
Light of what the carpenter referred to as—
"In my Father's house are many mansions."

Forget Me Not

Grandpa said when he was a little kid
When the big war raged and men and
Women all wore uniforms, he knew
Of a castle-like house on a huge private
Street that was frequented by hundreds of
Men in khaki and blue—he called them *soldier guys.*
There were White guys, and there were Black guys
There were big guys, short guys, and Latino guys
Bi-guys, straight guys, fast guys, fat guys, con guys
Farm guys, city guys, Navy guys, Army guys
Rich guys, poor guys, and wise guys
In-the-closet guys, and I-do-not-care guys
And I-am-curious guys, and what's-love-all-about guys
Movie star guys, and poetic guys, macho guys, and
Pretty guys, Ladies holding hands and smiling to and fro
A night of frolic and of love—for soon deployment
To combat zones the world over would yet demand
Much more—for some "a last full measure of devotion"
For a country that ridiculed their lifestyle.
Dedicated to the estimated one million gay men and women
Who served the US in all military services during World War II

Forgotten Longing

"What could it have been like?" he asks once again
A dreamland of buckskinned men and half-grown
Boys of oxen, dogs, and mules and what of Tejano
Ladies and their joys?
Do but we fantasize of a Texas long ago
Before the Alamo, and a slave boy named Joe
As you sit yet in your classroom in Boston
Struck by the drive of a man named Steve Austin
Few things grip and challenge a man to but wish
He was a Texan, for spirit and pride ebb and flow
And alas where history and legends still grow
Childhood heroes abound and battles play out
In the projectors of my mind, in these now
Twilight years I seem to see, the image of
Long ago, of you, the Alamo and a slave boy
Named Joe.

Forgotten Streams, Fields, and You

There is, on some such days as these, the
Gentle memory of a nearly-forgotten
Autumn breeze of fields of green and thousand
Years
Standing with your hand over your mouth
Blushing and laughing your dress flowing in the
Wind.

A weather-beaten wooden wagon
Abandoned now by a secret hidden stream
Where then century-before men wearing
Blue and gray fought and died for useless
False principles where you and I now played.

But memories of a half-century-plus ago
Where now strip malls, and highways take
The place of what used to be.

In my dreams of those bygone years and my
Adolescent tears, you smile again waving from
The shoreline of eternity.
A happy vivacious dog by your side.

Forgotten Texas Echo

The predawn Texas wind chased tumbleweeds
Across the makeshift dirt road the nocturnal
Critters made sounds now of retiring to their
Habitats leaving the dawning of a new day
To early risers and new sun.
He stood looking from the wooden
Planks of what once served as a strong
Porch-like structure leading into the
Now-weather-beaten hacienda, as he
Sipped his morning coffee.
The caffeine cleared his head from the
Long nights slumber he lit a cigarette
As the retiring distant sound of coyotes
Echoed in the colonies of his thoughts.
There was on his stove a large pot of beans
A big platter of biscuits, and always an extra
Pot of hot coffee, as was the case today as before
A migrant family from across the border tired
Hungry and afraid from the night before comes into view.
He smiles and waves them in with warmth.

Gentlemen, When We Are No More

(Ode to First-Line Defenders of 1941)

What might we hope that history brings
Later, in this huge scheme of things, will
The youth of today tell our story
Or perhaps remember those names of those
Who fell in glory and gore.

GENTLEMEN, WHEN WE ARE NO MORE.

When then a tsunami of aggressors sworn to
Enslave the world, we stood vigil as the first
Resisters, from Wake Island, Guam, and the isle
of the Philippines.

Who might sing our praises or carry our banner
Still on high
Might I say the years now have taken their toll
Upon these tired and tortured souls
Remember always we are brothers to the core.

GENTLEMEN, WHEN WE ARE NO MORE.

And when the child asks to read to me again, what happened
Way back then, and what was it they wrought?
Let our struggle nay be forgotten, shut not history's door.

GENTLEMEN, WHEN WE ARE NO MORE!

Ghost of a Gray Cat

There are noises that I hear from time to time
And my first thought being in this apartment
Complex the neighbors sound like they are
Fornicating in the next room.
Ah, should I choose to give up my space
and reside with another?
Or perhaps I already am, maybe the spirit of a
Departed one, a friendly visitor I should hope
Perhaps the ghost of a gray cat, who refused
To relinquish his time, thinking he can yet choose
Another space to inhabit with an accommodating staff.
I welcome him with open arms, remorseful for that
Day at the vets when my only option was
Euthanize but not separate the love from my life
I have grown now accustomed to otherworldly
Sounds about me
My demons from yesterday lay dead and flat
As I wake to the purring of the ghost of a gray cat.

Gluten Rising

They seek gratification from a God they cannot define
Yet strive for separation.
They look upon themselves with egotistical fervor
Slaughtering living things to devour.
They fight each other overpower and sway
Only to care little about the damage done.
Think you not, that we cannot see?
Know you not, time remains your erosion.
The flame of dominion, their hands do reach for
With eyes that cry for more, their obese bodies.
And minds lust but for more, matter not the price
Of others who perish of hunger, and die still in the
Streets for lack of sanitary conditions.
Hear you not that every soul craves her own salvation?
Your arrogance and delusion fills
They have invented the world they see.
Won't you listen but for a second, hear my call—
You, bastards, bastards all.

Go Not Willingly, My Love

He could only wonder in the bewilderment
of his yesterdays were now the years had gone.
slowly but surely the new reality began to encompass him.
He knew now that cold January wind
that whipped through the tall oaks was also
chilling the inner landscapes of his own being.
The memories began to show themselves
almost in movie projector fashion.
None but her own spirit of scores of vivacious
energies filled days packed with anticipation
new adventure, whatever else could have taken
him back to a hundred church basements and
potluck dinners.
What plea now could have kept her here?
"Go not so willingly, my love, into eternity's shadow."
The ghost of a warrior hound, so prepared
for battle (with me) came now to lead you
where my aching voice cried—"Go not willingly
into eternity's shadow."

Grandpa and Me

In those rolling hills of old Kentucky peppered
With coal mines and railways, I followed my grandpa
From hobo camps to the big city's soup lines to
A homestead cabin deep in the woods.

A *new deal* loan got him two mules a plow
A shotgun, fishing gear that brought in food, we grew
Our own garden and read the good book by coal oil
Lamp every night.

Sold our vegetables to up and coming vendors bought more
Land and hired some grateful wandering migrant workers
We sang songs by a bonfire late at night, nocturnal critters
Circled us just out of sight.

In those faraway memories of my youth and the passage
Of those years, I'm older now than grandpa was then, I
Done fought through two wars and built a dozen financial
empires.

Never found my parents proper, but in my twilight times
Now at the closing of each day, somewhere in the vastness
Of infinity I sense he hears my words.

"Grandpa, thank you,
Thank you. Thank you."

Heartbreak Blues Express

(I was thinking of legendary blues musician and writer Jesse Fuller when I wrote this. Maybe he channeled it to me.)

Packed all my gear, this hurt I'm feeling so bad
I gotta get on away from here
Went on down to dat old sad railroad station feeling
Pain and stress
Now I'm streamlin' on that Heartbreak Blues express
Call me home, baby, and I'll come a runnin' wait a see
Gets rid o'this emptiness and hurt inside a' me
Folks ever ask, "What's happened to me?" I guess
Tell em' I'm a ridin' dat Heartbreak Blues express
Conductor singin' a mournful song an' me a wonderin'
What went wrong, ain't thinkin' where dis train ends
Folks be lookin' and pointin' sayin' he done lost his mind
Over dat woman, thinkin' I could never love ya less
Gets me off this Heartbreak Blues express
If'n you baby done thrown you out and you all
Hurt and bothered, and there seems no way out
Come down here wit' me gets on board and
Feel blessed
On this, here's Heartbreak Blues express

In My Slumberland of Dreams

In my deep slumberland of dreams
The mystery that pulled me into this
Vortex of life staggers still understanding.
In the misty image of my yesterdays
I see again in dreams the promise of
A still new horizon with purple skies.
Yet the mind showers me with a hundred
Forms of fear baseless though they be
Surrounded still with faces masked by
questionable morals.
I find me once again running a marathon
Of sorts wind and rain, coyote-like critters
With predatory eyes watching me from the bushes.
The she-wolf, always the she-wolf, comforts
Me once more with wise counsel
My mind's eye sees the mama wolf carrying
Her cub by the scuff to safety.

Is It Fact or Is It History?

Who rides now through the midnight hours of
Sleeping hollows and gulley's and forgotten
Creek beds now dried and dusty
Silhouetted against a yellow moon on a steed
As black as the night she rides.

Born a princess and heiress to a kingdom beyond
Measure, she witnessed at age thirteen a slaughter of
Thousands of her countrymen, yet for the crime
Of being peasants who appealed only for food.

A shift inside began a slow unstoppable rage toward
Now her father and those of his court and henchmen all
She vowed silently within to avenge this terrible wrong
Learning the sword, bow, and use of battle axes at sixteen
She rode out of the palace gate.

She rallied the hillside peasants, organized trained them
In the craft of killing, ambushes, and taking no prisoners
The world titled her the female *Genghis Khan*
Her father put a price on her head.

For five years, there was freedom in the land
For oppression was stymied her lover a beautiful
Polynesian girl who fought by her side in many battles
Against the king's men and churchmen. Now betrayed
This young female warrior queen.

With help from her, the king's men set a trap, killing the
Young warrior queen, taking her head back to her father
Her lover was summoned to the king's court
Anxious to receive her reward.
Instead, she was sentenced to be burned at the stake for
Being involved in same-*sex sexual involvement.*

"Come on, old sport, is what you just told me a true story?
Actual history?" I asked.
"Actual history is a fairy tale. History is
just what we believe," he replied.

"HOLY CRAP!"

Rise Up, Rise Up

May I sing you a song of greatness
perhaps a song of who you are
rise now, as your brothers did before you.
The time is now, the voice is calling
the spirit is crying, now
rise, rise up your burden is but
a bump in the road.
Your rise lightens your load
rise up, rise up, engulf this moment
be not afraid for your destiny has
I sing been laid.
Your poetry is being written on the wind
rise, rise up
the masterful ones care not where you
child have been.
Take my hand, we will rise together and like
stallion and mare we shall ride in stride
oh, I sing, rise up, rise up.

School Day Memory

The school bus that carried us from Emerson Elementary
To Rock Spring School was full of sad-faced children who
Knew not of any reasoning as to why we were the ones chosen
For such a social experiment.

The driver chain-smoked cigarettes as the bus made grinding
Sounds as if to cry for us fifth graders (now of another day and
time) who were yet barely awake and dreaded this malady of
bussing.
The stench of the slaughter houses hung in the air, the corrals
Holding the cattle bit at our abdomens, they too, having been
Chosen for something they could not comprehend.
The large castle-like institution stood alone in an inner
City flattened landscape, we felt cold, empty, and afraid
The Rock Spring kids taunted us, bullied us, and hurled
Names at us.

Filling us with an even more silent plea
To be anywhere but here.

Song of Life

This new year of the many I have seen tells me
This is but the beginning of joy and bliss yet to be.

I have come to thee, oh, life as an entity that some
Day transforms itself to new horizons taking us to
The very shores of eternity.

To meet old souls and rejoice again, as we did then
I sing of this song of life and cherish her monocles
And yet proclaim her gifts of pain and joy.

But what is this song I sing, it proclaims only
New and blissful awakenings from this labor
Of strife, child this song of life.

The fearless proclaim four scores thrice there is
No death, only new levels of life.

Song of the Warrior

With Washington, I crossed Delaware that cold and wintery night
And felt the frostbite and nagging hunger that did surge that winter
At Valley Forge.
I closed ranks with Andrew Jackson in
New Orleans and held old glory
High and served with men that day who weren't too proud to die.
I stood with buckskinned men and boys
on the walls at the Alamo of
Every race and creed were we, song of the warrior, yes that was me.
I marched beside Lee and Grant and saw
Lee raise the saber in his hand
As the South made her last stand.
I stood next to Custer at the Little Bighorn,
watched the end as it came
Near, as history judged us, they would both sneer and cheer.

Ode to the Passage of Time

Said the master to the slave, "I have my Jezebels
And my Southern belles, I have my wife and
Mistress too, but all in all I sing, I still have you."

The night wind howls and whispers to thee an omen
Of a long-ago age when *God was a woman.*

The slave could but dream of liberation from
His hell while the women folk of the day
Could but hope to *marry well.*

Where now are the warrior queens of a bygone
Rein, dare I call upon the goddesses of war men
Rule, or is that but an illusion of the mind.

Today I feel their eyes on me at work
When I walk to the coffee maker
Somewhat regrettable for they wonder
Is she at all fuckable?

But then, here's to Walking Buffalo Woman
Who during the battle at Little Bighorn took?
Pleasure in mutilating the bodies of the wounded
Soldiers, after they had killed her children.

The Bellevue House

I saw you for sale in old Maplewood you stood
elegant as you always have
made new on the inside you again drew me to you.
You felt the anguish and the pain, your timbers shook
your shutters trembled and fell.
You sank into oldness, antiquity in sad need of repair.
When we began to heal, alas so did you.
You sprung with us. Your light did glow.
You became a showplace of pride and healing.
Bellevue house, never should we have left you.
May I (alone now) have you back?
I will be home.

The Diner at Newstead

One of the few all-night eateries in St. Louis in 1957
and one where when my friend came over to spend
the night, we pooled our nickels together and spent a
great deal of time drinking soda and playing the juke box.
Centered between a shoeshine parlor and a liquor store
and street cars on rails that rumbled up and down olive
street and down the busy thoroughfare
their flourished *Gaslight Square*
Was there a better time to be fifteen alive and fine and
the first time I heard Johnny Cash sing "I Walk the Line"
In all the joy of those teenage years of bliss and beauty
I recall the vision of a girl named Judy.
In a time of condominiums, strip malls, and super clover highways
I only wonder what happened to the diner on Newstead and Olive.

My Visitor

Not so long ago, I had a dream of an angel
Visited me smiling and joyful.
I vaguely sensed I knew the angel from a time now passed
The angel expressed a beauty and ambiance
Of love. I knew was not of this world.
My first thought was of course one of gratitude.
Of which he or she at once offered to discuss.
I explained I could not ever talk to God
Without first expressing how grateful I was
Whereas we both went down on bended knees
And I began my gratitude list.
Soon after my angelic visitor expressed
Time in the eternal world is not your world
You have made time of the essence, I must be
On my way.
Do I not know you said I? Have we not crossed
Paths before?
My visitor responded, perhaps in a hundred different
Church basements, potluck dinners, a
can plant, we take many forms
Many forms?
I woke up, the ghost of a gray cat walking across my chest.

Ode to a Lady Poet

Who might we be moved and touched
By the tenor voice and notes that hang
In the quadrangle and deepest part of our yesterdays
Or be it the poet's pen that can cut like a
Sword or soothe again a broken heart
Or bring to life a love that died or her
Verse that resonates within
The verse, the words, the rhyme though
You know me not, intuitively I know
They were penned but only for you.
If I could see her, I could love her.
For I know her now, through verse
Is she of free spirit, wild as the wind
I imagine blowing through her hair
Could she desire me, as I do her?
The tragedy of verse is it leaves true love hanging
I scribe these lines to a lady poet
Of whom I dearly love, though she
She—will never know it

Ode to Annie Oller

One who carried herself in reverence
Above and beyond whose love I carried
Yet never donned
One who was considerate and kind
Might I say Annie Oller was a friend of mine?

One whose eyes and smile lit up the world
Whose energy and inspiration never grew old
One of whom I feel is yet near time to time
Might again I say
Annie Oller was a friend of mine.

Might I sing of thee again, as I so did then
Under a trillion nocturnal stars and dying
Embers of a trout lodge campfire I sense
Comfort of having known her
In my soul, does she shine
You know, Annie Oller was a friend of mine.

Ode to Joyce Kilmer

What, sir, might I begin to add to
the sacredness of trees that you
have not so elegantly penned.
You saw with the poet's eye that which
I struggle so hard to see.
To feel the beauty and sacredness of a tree
a gift endowed to but a few. When I look upon
a thousand-year-old oak, my thoughts revert to thee.
My hero poet who I strive so much to follow
might I feel the sacred rhythm of the tree
humble poet that I be.
That fateful day you fell upon a battlefield
and they buried you under the trees you so immortalized.
Should you have lived, and taught, and wrote
ignored the war that no poet wants, might we have met—

Odyssey Lost

The smell of coffee from the campfires
Mixed with the cold Montana wind
Permeated his nostrils
Images of men in buffalo hide coats
And knee-high riding boots pulled at
The bridles of reluctant pack mules
From the distant plain the sunrays
Peaked through buttermilk clouds
As the last of the nocturnal critters
Made their way to their habitats
Dark-faced men saddled their mounts
As a sense of déjà vu encompassed him
Visions in slumberland tortured him he
Was again reminded he was lost in a world
Where he did not belong
The ghost of a gray cat licked his hand.

Places In My Heart

There are places in my heart that give me pause,
There are places in my heart that fill the emptiness.
Within, you know, there are places in my heart I can never go again,
And there are places in my heart that hold you still.
There are places in my heart the poet's pen can only fill,
There are places in my heart where you are there.
With a southern breeze still whispering through your hair,
There are places in my heart of all that ever,
Was, and all that's ever been of Afghan hounds.
And long-haired cats and baby robins once again,
There are places in my heart of endless hills and streams.
And thousand-year-old oaks and pines and no fences for,
A thousand miles, where you changed me from a boy into a man.
There is a place in my heart where you stand,
With rising mist about you, daffodils, and things like that,
By your side, the ghost of a gray cat.
There's a place in my heart that promises me we will meet again.

Raven's Echo

The ceiling fan blades turn slowly
circulating as I lie and watch me
mind is captivated.
Painted blades of an artist's hand
now long gone, yellow roses of
swirling air and a sweet breeze of
my used-to-bes.
My restless soul longs for you
still again, as it so did then a longing
for what was somewhere when
the raven watches dubiously from the oak
the ghost of a gray cat purrs in my ear.

Redneck Lesbian

Now she serves up whiskey down at the
Roadhouse Grill and Bar them good ole boys
Say she can play a mean guitar.
Dancing on the bar in miniskirt, boots, and
Cowboy hat and a leather shirt singin' to
Her ex, "How ya like me now?"
Now she got a Dixie flag on her truck
She says, "It ain't coming down no how"
As good a lookin' as any girl in Texas
Appeals now too to both sexes
(If ya so need to know)
Pretty as they come, despised by some
Carries a Colt 45 and can outshoot any
Man alive, yeah, such charm, but she's got
Linda tattooed on her arm.
Dimples on her chin, long silky black hair
Bangs coming out from her cowboy hat
Grandpa was here he be letting out a rebel yell.
Her true love at the Houston playhouse
And theater, a leading lady thespian
But, Lord, let me tell ya how I love that
Redneck Texas lesbian.

Restless Heart

What was the intuitive pull that kept him awake at night
this attraction was so compelling that took him on long
midnight rides on a steed who in the depth of his being
knew and understood him better than the very society
he felt so trapped in.
Somewhere he knew not where someone had whispered
the need to have a longing for more, like a hollowness
within, a desire for some unknown fulfillment that these
nocturnal rides through thickened forests filled the emptiness
if only temporally.
The unquenchable thirst for nature in her untamed origin
engulfed him in the present moment he was gifted
with experiencing a total *oneness* and connectedness
with every living creature that ever was.
The freshness, always the freshness, of wildness
the grizzly, she-wolves with her column of cubs, so
close he felt, yet so far even with the oneness
was there not a legend somewhere from his boyhood
did not a young man mate with a wolf, a grizzly?
He sat upon the stallion's back, on a ridge overlooking
the canyon below, how blessed yet can another be for
he, at last, knew he was where he longed to be.

Legend in Our Time

Aw, what literary works bear your footprint
Of touching the human soul. Should
Shakespeare or Hemingway achieved
Anything close (I think not)
Whose written words of Texas echo yet
In the canyons and open plains of yesteryear
That filled my boyhood dreams.
You, who penned heroes and examples of
Unsung heroes that we dared to imitate
(Or not)
That even the villains drew us to their nefarious
Ways and actions heroes and villains both fought
Their inner demons
From *Lonesome Dove* to *Brokback Mountain*
None in whoever scribed Western history
Has accomplished anything near your literary
Genius
Thank you for the journeys into life itself as
Your characters knew it to be
Oh, thank you, Larry McMurtry.

Desperate Echo

There was a time in his life that was now more
Of a blur, along with a misty drenched young ghost that
Challenged his senses that only he could see.
Feeling maybe there was a hint of completeness to be had
The ghost of his youth was always near.
In his dreams, he would come, a young khaki
Clad man whose eyes were scared and spoke of
A bewilderment beyond his comprehension.
There seemed no content in separation.
The fetal position he slept in doorways and
Park benches with the cold empty hole within
That enough whiskey could never fill.
The VA doctors told him, "Your war has been over for decades
Get on with life, at least you returned."
"What about them that did not?"
One day the young man in his visions
would reclaim him, one day they
Would both return to a desolate road on
Bataan and discover another body
From another time, another war, at long last reunited.

Spirit Chimes

Inner chimes that tinkle and remind
Me again of an ongoing divinity that
Encompasses my essence that nay
Will I ever walk alone.

Chimes of spirit keep on singing
Chimes of spirit keep on soaring
Might I sing of thee to the sky above
Might I praise thee again, as perhaps
I did then.

Sing now your sacred song, sing
Again, of your healing grace, while
I raise my arms in gratitude of the
Salvation and forgiveness, we already
Know.

Chimes of spirit that resonate throughout
My being, that light my way and lift me with
New joys, and promises of new horizons, and
A never-forgotten messiah.

Spirit chimes sing for the least of us, homeless children
Abandoned animals, the down trod and war-weary ones
Chimes of spirit let us move as one in love and light
Praise be yours—

Broken Sayonara
Timeline Japan—September 1945

Was little doubt the beast of war had
Left her mark on his once-beautiful
Homeland, where hunger and death had
Taken their toll.

A corpse-like stillness now gripped
The rubble ruined city blocks, save
For the distant sound of airplanes
Landing with occupation troops.

The agonizing brutality of war weakened him
He walked the road alone, in his shirt he clung
To a rising sun battle flag, he promised his dying
Comrade in the last battle in the Philippines he
Would return it to his family.

The confusion of war made such a request unfulfilled.

Children, orphans of the massive firebombing raids
Came out of the rubble, now, like so many stray
Dogs and cats, he recalled before the war.

He gave them the last of his chocolate bars
The American soldiers had given him.

Was like the old childhood story, the lonely
Lost goose flying alone, an emptiness gripped
His insides, these sights sent a chill down
His spine and left a tingling in his testicles.

Somewhere now, in his imagination, all must
Be joined, somewhere—somewhere the ghosts
Of Bataan
were now embracing the orphans of Hiroshima
It cannot be otherwise.

Covenant of Blood
(Gallows Hill)

A ghost-like wind sweeps about my feet
As I walk on hallowed ground and ask
Myself again are they remembered anywhere
By any poet's quill?
Here upon which is called *Gallows Hill*
1692 they say was the year Christians stood in silence
And shed nay a tear, daring not utter even a prayer
As six young girls condemned to hang innocent though
They be.
What now had one of thee been me? Oh, the Christian
Blood and tongue were still
That day on Gallows Hill.
What energy draws me here, an inner voice I cannot tell
That you unjustly died by what they cried was God's holy word.
Might I but utter, curse thee adamant Christians, has your fear
Been lessoned, your diseases cured, your sick minds healed?
I dismount my nervous steed on bended knee I offer a prayer
To the six young girls—condemned by robe covered, jewelry laden
Puritan, pompous snakes disguised as humans.
No thrill—
Here on Gallows Hill.

Day after Infamy[1]

Word has it we are at war, our huge silver
Bomber flies over the Philippine Sea on its first war patrol
Smoke bellows up in the distance as fires continue
Burning from yesterday's unexpected strike.

In an instant, we are under fire from incoming
Zeros their guns striking us like so much hail
They buzz about us, I see a pilot, goggles
Scarf, and helmet, a mustached-face looking sternly on.

Two of our gunners lie in a pool of blood, my copilot
Humped over in his seat the cockpit smoking and fire
Dancing around my feet.

My navigator screams over the radio, to hold steady
As ever more bullets tear into our bomber.
They all press home their attack as we lose altitude
The fire making its way up my arms and chest licking
My head and face, the blue wide ocean rushing up
To meet us.

The Pacific waters extinguish the flames
The bomber sinks under the waves, the
Coolness of the water washing over my face
And body, giving me my last earthly pleasant memory.

---

[1]   Dedicated to Sam Merritt, United States Army Air Corps killed in action over
   the Philippine Sea, December 9, 1941

Faro Friend

Why does the faro cat cry?
Does she long for times of
Innocence or alleyways of
Her yesterdays?

Her litter struggles for a tit at feeding
Time as her eyes tell all.
She climbs the tree in my yard.

Scanning the territory, she has
Claimed for her own.
She searches with dubious eyes
Freshly placed barrels of trash or easy
Prey.

My draw to her, I do not comprehend
As I place one more bowl of cat food
In my yard of which she partakes
Vigorously.

On moon-lit nights as the city sleeps
She rendezvouses again with the ghost
Of a gray cat.

Mirrored Image

In the misty zone upon my awakening
I catch in my mind's eye a smiling face
Of innocence surrounded in an aura of
White light.

For but briefly I ask were we together
In my dreams, now perhaps bidding
Me ado as I return from slumberland?

During yet my days of struggle of climbing
And stumbling falling back in a sea of wonder
Side stepping life's booby traps so often
The destiny of this journey.

What yet gives sway to somewhere that
Smiling face of innocence seen by my eyes
Only.
From whence she comes I know not
Yet have I heard said, "Angels appear in
All guises—classrooms, boardrooms
Bathrooms, war rooms (and can plants
on occasion)—thee gives me grace."

Ode to a World War II Marine
(Timeline 1943)
(The Cost)

The band played *semper fidelis* on the day
of graduation from boot camp
Had my picture taken with Dad and Mom in my
uniform they beamed with pride that day.

A short visit back home, the corner drug store with my
High school sweetheart sharing a malt, the neighborhood
Kids cheering and circling about me, touching my dress blues
As they gawk in awe.

Soon I am on board a transport ship sailing in the
South Pacific the fever pitch of my first combat
Fuels my patriotism as our destination comes in view
The island of Tarawa.

Descending the net to the landing craft
The excitement in me escalated.
As the sounds of battle grew, the boatswain lowered the ramp
I sprung forward as randomly as the enemy mortar shell that
Struck me.

My body parts were collected, identified, and thrown in
A pine box draped with the flag of a country I loved,
killed by an enemy I never saw, a letter of condolences
to my family from a general I never met.

The Travelers

There are places I have walked
With souls I have loved.
And serenaded by life's gifts from
Songbirds and butterflies to
Honeybees.
There are places I have sat with the
Muse of many ages, from rolling boxcars
To horse barns and campfires of the
Plains.
Child, don't you know I have shared my
Handouts to stray dogs and cats
Should you have walked my path, would you
Have been the better for it? I know not.
Can thee sing of Ivy League schools and halls
Of scholarly academia.
Where then may we meet? Perhaps the far side of Jordan
And what would God say to thee, and he to me?
I have created both thee in my likeness and image.
And by me thee deeds are weighed.

Rain and Leaves

'Tis the rain this misty morning
That falls upon the leaves that
Mysteriously feed the inner
Landscapes of my being.

An echoing refrain that gently
Begs a question of why we are
Here?

'Twas one-day millenniums now past
That God created these universes
These worlds, perhaps thousands
We know not of.

The rain that falls from the leaves
Sing a poetic verse to all things for purpose, value
Encompassed by the wonder of creation
Again, I ask our God we both adore (DEAR READER).

Lift again my vision that I may see beyond my ego.
While the rain falls gently upon the leaves
And the breeze (the breath of God) kisses
My face.

Sings the Happy Soul

Sings now my happy soul for what this new day brings
The slowly melting away of a buttermilk sky as sunbeams
And rays dance their way into this new dawn, peppered
With distant southbound geese chirping and talking in
A language lost to me.

Sings my happy soul for critters in the forest at play
Sings yet my happy soul for gratitude that abounds
Sings again my happy soul where the water meets
The sand.

And the lion that now lies with the Lamb.
Oh, sings my happy soul when I see a father
Embracing his own son's son.

What better symphony feeds my ears and visual
Than the creator's own handiwork.

Sings my happy soul that heaven opened its gates
And I found you, as you did me.

Sings my happy soul I thirst no more
I thirst no more, sings again my happy soul.

Where My Heart Has Been

Watching the morning blades of sunlight
Fashion their way through the pines and oaks
Again.
Oh, do I think of the places and times my
Heart has been.

Seeing you in the morning breeze at your
Easel capturing on your campus natures
Splendor.

Was it not the symphony of a hundred-plus
Forty-three songbirds, or the morning salutations of
Heaven's lost echo of souls faraway yet near

Do I dream of way back when, oh, you know
Of places where my heart has been.

How so sweet this new day that gives sway
To gratitude, that on your journey through
Life, you came my way.

Short Stories

Noun. A piece of prose fiction, usually under ten thousand words.

A Short Story of Love and War

I do not know if this happened. I do not know if it did not happen. I only know it is a true story.

The time line is February 1945; the place is the volcanic island of "Iwo Jima," where some of the bitterest fighting took place between American marines and Japanese military forces. Before the island was secured and fighting ceased, seven thousand Americans would be dead as well as seventeen Japanese soldiers.

Anyone who was there, even to the end of their lives, never escaped the haunting remembrances of Iwo Jima. As all had a story, this is one of those stories.

The young marine realized he had a sudden burning in his right knee; looking down, he saw blood pulsating from his wound; his leg went limp as he stumbled down a ravine onto an open road, which remarkably had a few small trees and bushes lining its dirt road. His head was spinning as his pain became excruciating; he could not reach his kit that held the morphine syringe.

He yelled in fear as he felt two arms, one under each shoulder, pulled him upward, dragging him out of the road and pulling him behind the hedges. He opened his eyes and saw what appeared to be the face of a huge dog.

"Jesus Christ," he blurted out. The huge dog laughed. "No, I wouldn't go that far." The dogs's paws, which were more like human hands, fumbled to find gauze, bandages, and morphine. "It's all right," the talking dog said. "You will be okay."

"What the f—— is going on here!" The wounded marine screamed, trying to scramble backward; his wound was painful enough he fell back toward the huge animal.

"You're a f——g talking dog 'less I'm losing my GD mind. Oh god, I hurt."

"Yeah, you got a nasty wound. I've been patching up a lotta you humans this day."

"I ain't never saw no talking dog, and your huge, big as man. You can't be real." The marine began to sob, burying his face in the dog's fur.

"We have to get someone to carry you to the aide station. If your enemy finds you now, they will kill you."

"Yeah, lousy sons of bitches," the marine replied.

"I resent that," the dog replied. "Sons of men is more appropriate. Dogs did not start this war."

"I gotta be losing my f——g mind. I ain't gonna make it home."

"Hear me," the dog responded. "You start thinking about home, love, and all it means to you."

"Love? This is f——g war."

"Someday, someway, you humans will have to learn war is not a solution. It cannot endure."

"I'm leaving you here. You are safe. Keep your thoughts on love and home. Forget not our encounter."

The medics were tending him when one spoke to the other, "Damn, that thing looked like a big ape that left here. I mean, it was fast-moving."

"It was a dog," the wounded marine said.

"Well, whatever it was, it stopped your bleeding and probably saved your life."

On February 23, 1945, Joe Rosenthal (photographer) took the most famous picture of World War II—the planting of the American flag on Mount Suribachi by five young marines and one naval medic. This image has been viewed by millions over the decades, remains in history books, symbolic of the marine corps, and embedded in war memorials the world over. What was not reported was a few feet from the flag raising was the dead carcass of an exceptionally large dog said to be the size of a man with limbs that resembled humans.

Word and rumor had it that the unusually huge dog was making its way toward three wounded marines when it was felled by small arms fire.

Dysfunctional Illusion

My first encounter with cowboys and Indians came on the silver screen at the *plaza picture show* on Clara and Etzel in St. Louis. This was post-World War II, and many of the Westerns had been made in the 1930's *Tom Mix, Johnny Mack Brown, Roy Rogers.* The one thing these movies all had in common was all the cowboys, and most all the Indians were White, yeah, Caucasian. And at that time (pre-civil rights movement), we had no inkling there ever existed any *Negro cowboys and Indians.*

And I, having started kindergarten, knew very little about different races of people. Save for one night while waiting in line to buy a ticket at the plaza, the ticket lady refused a friend a ticket because she thought he was Black. Well, this caused a bit of a ruckus, and I was able to overhear the conversation. Milan, who was a brown-skinned Italian boy, kept telling the ticket lady, "I am not one of them. I am not one of them."

He was about to cry.

One of the kids ran to Milan's house and told his mother what was going on up at the show.

His mom came up there very livid and cussed the ticket lady out. The manager got involved and finally settled the issue everyone agreeing Marvin was not Black but a darker-than-usual Italian. The manager apologized to Milan's mom.

However, getting back to my original subject of never seeing any Black faces in Western movies, I ask a teacher later what all the freed slaves did after the Civil War. She vaguely hinted at two United States Cavalry regiments that fought Indians out West. The rest is history. From that moment forward, I became an advocate of African American history.

I discovered that many Western movie stars, especially Will Rogers, openly talked about spending time with Negro cowboys, and they taught him how to rope and ride when he was young. (And Will Rogers never minced words.) He spoke exactly what was on his mind. Later, I learned most cattle drives and ranges were spearheaded by Black men. I have to remember being a cowboy was not all it was cracked up to be on the silver screen.

They slept in the open, on the dirt rocky ground, and had a strict diet of hardtack and beans. The work was intense; the weather was unpredictable. Often, there were Indian attacks and rustlers who needed to be fought off. It was not a job for everyone, but given the choice of staying in the South where racism was an ever-increasing force or going North where the *labor movement* was ever fearful of former slaves taking the jobs, many African American men and their families moved West.

Where cattle barons both European and American hired them in on trail drives, many began to learn the technique of the cowboy: roping, shooting, chasing strays, and riding this life that offered a great deal more than remaining in a region known for its racism against former slaves.

There was a degree of discrimination and segregation that existed in the cattle country but will not obscure the fact that the Negro cowboy did not display conspicuous abilities and contributed greatly to the cattle industry and the settling of the West.

They were often paid the same as their White counterparts, and many horse breakers, ropers, and cooks remain in their positions of considerable prestige in the *Western cowboy culture.*

Moses

People were coming and going, and it was not as if the road to Nacogdoches was empty; for now, it appeared the oppressor was unstoppable. He moved as swiftly as he could, a makeshift knapsack and his musket strapped across his back with the skin of a wild boar, serving as a strap.

A wild raven followed him from San Antonio. It had been four days since he left; somehow, he had an intuitive sense they were all dead by now.

It was evident the population had heard the Alamo was gone, and panic was gripping the Texicans. He continued. In time, he would be called a coward. In time, he would testify to the new republic who had been with him.

In those last days, so the new republic might compensate their families, he opened a butcher shop in Nacogdoches and said he never regretted getting out. He said he just wasn't ready to die.

Devil or Angel

The dancing of the waves from where I stand
The sea breeze gently throws the mist on my face
As I taste and sense the salty aroma of the ocean
Front.

What is this endless marauder we call change?
Must we welcome this sometimes-rude intruder?
Of which I never am aware of what this bringer
Named change will present me.

It is you, my pursuer my shadow my never ending
Challenge of life, off times camouflaged in the
Unexpected veil of shock and awe.

Change, you have given me all that I ever loved
And have taken all that I ever cherished with only
A settling attitude of "oh, hum, change, she is the
Only thing that remains constant"

Leaving me with the only option to embrace thee
For to resist you is a losing battle the never ending
Challenge of you.

Resist her, embrace her—either way she will remain.

Each New Dawn

Seems like each sunrise, or cloudy day for that matter, is one more day in my life. I can chalk up with gratitude. Looking back over my life, I see that I choose to put this body and mind most of the abuse and pain through over the years. It's a wonder I lasted this long.

So each and every day, now that I awaken to, I at once feel gratitude and look so forward to doing the next right thing, with the death of Steve Jobs. And hearing many of his lectures on life and death—in particular, the one he made at Stanford University graduating class (I don't recall the year)—did move me.

All in truth, don't wait to tell your family you love them. Repair old friendships, and do the things today you would do if this were your last day of life. Now that really hit me, and it delivered an awareness that was driven home by my visit to the Emergency Room for bleeding gum. That could have been a lot worse. And my resentments and intolerance of other people's behaviors in their life have little to do with me. My trying to control the lives of others and harbor anger for the way they live only add to my conflict where I squander hours that could have been well spent on a more positive mode.

Now, a lot of us have been reading inspirational books for years and doing Pollyanna-type affirmations, and some of us have even taken our prayers and meditations for granted, but there is nothing in life like a wakeup call that grabs your awareness and soul like "Wow, I could have been doing so much with my life." Again, I am faced with life's challenges of *letting go* as another good friend who is in the hospital with pancreatic cancer and has opted to not have any further treatments his faith and his giving so freely to others has taught me much in the short three years I have known him. His faith sustains him as it did Ginny in her last months. It is that peace and calmness in the eye of life's worst storms that winners and champions are made.

And at times in my life, as a constant observer, I know that it is that kind of faith and peace that I still long for. Quoting Breaker Morant, I will close by saying, "Live each day like it's your last, for one day you will be right."

Feline Echo (A Texas Tale)

"I mean, not to be a native Texan, you know a lot about our history," he said.

Motioning for the waiter to refill our coffee cups.

"Comes from being, an amateur historian," I said, "living through the Davey Crockett frenzy of the early fifties."

"Well, least you're not trying to rewrite our history."

"See," I went on "I always learn more. I was really taken when I heard the story about Ruby and CC, the two Alamo cats."

"Yeah, well," he said, "if ya feed a faro cat, they going to hang around. What may I ask is so special about cats hanging around after ya feed them? Ya said ya was taken by that story."

"Well, I not only study history. I research it to the core."

"That right?" He pulled out a bandana, wiping the sweat from his forehead. I could tell he was beginning to wonder why my conversation was drifting from the cradle of Texas Liberty to a couple of cats.

"Ya know," he said. "How'd folks live without AC in Texas?"

The waiter refilled our cups. He took a sip. "Never too hot for coffee in the morning though."

"See, my daughter took me over to the research center in San Antonio at the Alamo, and I ask one of the *daughters of the Republic* about why so much emphasis on these two cats?" By this time, my Texas friend was looking at me a bit dubious. "She told me that extensive research gave convincing evidence a stray cat had been in the Alamo for nearly twelve days of the glorious thirteen and had become quite sociable and friendly with the Alamo defenders as well as the women and children.

"On the morning of the final assault, the cat was said to be offering much loving comfort to the defenders. When the battle was over and all the Texans dead, this cat was moving about the corpses as if he was searching for someone.

"As he was moving about, a Mexican soldado thought he was a Texan still alive. He raised his musket to shoot him, then realized it was just a cat. A very superstitious officer yelled. 'It is a rebel insurgent. Kill him.' So you know, I just wonder if there is a, like, ghostly connection maybe between these cats?"

"Sir, I am a sixth-generation Texan. I heard a lot of Alamo stories in my day, but that one takes the cake. I know you're a poet and a writer, and all I can say is you got one hell of an imagination."

He got and exited the door, leaving me with the bill.

First Taste of Texas

It was a long drive in the U-Haul from Atlanta to Hockley, Texas, that November in 2012. My son-in-law had driven the whole way nonstop, save for coffee and bathroom breaks.

My son had passed away in August, and my daughter had pleaded with me to come to Texas for us to be closer.

My son-in-law and I were both exhausted when we crossed the Louisiana State Line and saw the sign "Welcome to Texas." It was time for a bathroom break and coffee as we had a few more miles to go.

The big all-night Exxon quick shop and gas was busy enough for 4:00 a.m., I thought. My son-in-law filled the tank. (We relived ourselves.) I grabbed some snacks, coffee, and a couple of bottles of water when a young man behind me mentioned to the cashier, "I want to pay for this gentleman," nodding at me.

He was tall, a cowboy with Stetson boots, Western attire. *Quite young*, I thought. I started to say, "Oh no, son. That's okay."

But he had already paid and said, "Welcome to Texas, sir."

I told my son-in-law, and we both went to thank him, but he was back in a white pickup truck and gone.

I tried to put it all together. Angel, spirit guide—this was my first taste of Texas, a kind smiling young cowboy who I never had the pleasure of meeting again.

From then on, I knew I loved Texas.

Flashback

"Much-obliged," John said as he dismounted the horse. The Black family offered them coffee and beans, filling their tin plates with cooked meat.

"What is this?" Lil Jake asked.

"Ain't nothing ya mama ever made," John replied. "Be grateful we getting it."

The Negro family told them of being slaves to a large landowner in North Carolina, and when the union army came, they had packed up what belongings they had and left the plantation, heading north.

Around the fire that night, John explained to them they were returning confederate soldiers and that Lee had surrendered to Grant at Appomattox Court House in Virginia and that they (the boys) were not slave owners, never had been, and did not believe in the institution of slavery. John had advised the family to continue to move north as it appeared many distraught Southern former slave owners would want to reap vengeance on the Negro population. They (the boys) had chosen to fight with the confederacy because Georgia was home.

At this time, however, the boys were still a good ways from Atlanta and Columbia, South Carolina, where the true aftereffects of Sherman's march would be visible for years and generations to come. The idea of a nation coming together and healing itself would have a terrible twist on how returning confederates would envision this idea after seeing Atlanta and parts of South Carolina.

But tonight, the boys were grateful for the hospitality of this family of former slaves. John had shot some squirrels and rabbits and had given them to the family. They cooked up some possum and gave the boys some extra potatoes and, again, filled their canteens.

From a local stream, they fed their horses and mounted them heading closer to Georgia now.

Once crossing over into Georgia, they encountered hundreds of returning confederate soldiers, mostly walking, crippled, wounded men. Their battle flags were rolled up, wearing frowns that spoke of a determination that was now broken and defeated.

A few wagons, pulled by starved and tired mules, carried some of the more severely wounded.

The boys joined in the long procession going into Atlanta. There was a wooden roof canopy up the road. Three men were dishing up grits and beans. Some of the returning men stopped and asked for some food. As the boys rode by, Henry and John glanced over at them.

One of the men dishing up the vittles raised his ladle. "Get outta here, ya damn beggar. Ya got nothing to barter with. Get back in that line. I ant got no use for rebels anyway."

Seeing this, John and Henry dismounted and walked over to the stand that was dishing up the food. "What's this about?" John asked.

The man with the ladle looked at John. "Ain't none yore affair, boy. We down here helping to maybe git y'all up and running again."

Henry looked and saw a box of watches and rings behind the three men. "Hell, ya'll ant nothing but damn carpetbaggers."

The man put down his ladle. "You kind a young to be talking to me like that."

John threw the blanket off the Spencer, while Henry pulled the colt revolver out, pointing it at the carpetbagger's nose. John was covering the two men. "I outta kill both ya'll right now."

"Git your ass's down the road and leave that box of watches and rings you stole from our men and leave all your food stuff." Henry barked.

"Mister, we gotta right to be here we businesspeople. The union troops guaranteed us protection," one of the men said. "Besides, none of ya'll supposed to have weapons."

"I killed my first man when I was twelve," Henry went on. "And I got a hanker to kill you now."

"Better git movin," John added. "He meant what he said."

The three men moved quickly down the road.

"Come on, ya'll." John yelled at the long line of men. "Line up and get some of this grub. Yankee grub beats no grub."

Many starving men ate that day, and the boys moved on after dispensing the watches and personal items back to the original owners. They kept moving, knowing the carpetbaggers would report them to the nearest union cavalry unit.

Entering Atlanta (what was left of it) filled their abdomens with ice cubes and left a tingling emptiness in their tentacles.

Not a structure was left standing, and many of the buildings still smoldered. There were scattered union squads of cavalry that patrolled the ruins and infantrymen who were camped in clearings. This day, the boys saw sights they would remember for a lifetime. Some of the union soldiers were sharing their rations with former slaves. A few White children were clinging to the former slaves that tended them. It did seem more and more union troops were pouring into the city.

The boys looked at each other in dismay and bewilderment. When Lee had gone into Pennsylvania, they did not burn the farms or ravish the town of Gettysburg. How dare that beast Sherman call himself a professional soldier? He would never again be thought of anything other than a murderer and pillager in the South. It was this sight of Atlanta that the boys wished for a brief moment. They had gone on fighting after Lee surrendered.

Riding around the smoldering ruins of Atlanta, the boys took care not to draw attention to themselves. John remembered their saddlebags were filled with hardtack and crackers with beans. So the only real issue was getting to Talking Rock.

Word had it the train tracks to Talking Rock were intact as Sherman had captured some of the Southern railroads and used them for his own troop movements.

They rode to the one depot outside Atlanta, which was sweltering with federal troops. Careful to leave the Spencer wrapped in the blanket, John walked up to the station master who was a union officer standing with a clipboard in his hand.

"Sir, my friends and I are trying to return to Pickens County, and someone said we maybe can get a ride on this train?"

"You returning rebs?" The officer asked.

"Yes, sir," John answered.

"Well, have you guys signed the pledge?"

"Pledge? What pledge is that?"

"Not ever to take up arms against the union again," the officer replied. "And we then provide transportation to get you back home."

"See, we already made our way from Virginia, and it's only fifty more miles."

"Boy, you all look a might young to have served in the Confederacy even though I know they were taking 'em in younger all the time."

"Well, we were there nearly all the battles since 1862," Henry said from his horse.

"What ya gonna do with the horses if I let ya ride back on the train?"

"They were good companions. Like to bring 'em along."

"Ya gonna need 'em for the spring planting?" the officer asked.

"Well, sure will know somebody that does."

"Looks like you Southerners are all gonna have to pull together, after that mess you made," the officer went on. "Let me go fetch those pledge papers for you to sign, then well get you on the next train, minus those horses."

"Yeah, well, look, sir. Save yourself the trouble. Making it this far from Appomattox, we want sign'n no pledge papers now. We gonna go ahead and make it the rest of the way."

"Union army is going to be in Georgia a long time, boys. Best sign these pledge papers," the officer said.

John looked at Henry and Lil Jake. "Which way home ya'll?"

"North," Henry said.

"Still took us three days," John said. "At about fifteen miles a day. But at least we was home."

"Know they talk about the war with Spain, the Philippine Insurrection, and that thing on the Mexican border, and the one in France, but I'm telling ya, Henry, there wasn't no war like our war."

"Yeah." Henry agreed. "They gonna be talking 'bout our war till the end of time."

"They still folk's comin' down from the north askin' questions 'bout why we seceded and why we fought," John added. "Some sayin' we were still wrong to own slaves. Hell, we never owned no slaves. I remember a fella from New York, claiming we were in all sorts of violations. I said, 'Hey, don't be pointing your finger at me 'cause my family never owned slaves.'

"Then he says, 'Well, you fought for the confederacy, so you just as guilty.' I finally told that idiot, if he didn't git movin', I was gonna lose the hounds on him."

"Well, ya know," John continued, "ever thought of what ya was gonna do when ya gets too old to stay out here all by yaself?"

"Well," Henry replied, "my granddaughter and her husband said fer me to come stay with 'em in Atlanta."

"Hope it won't never come to that with me," John said.

"But you know our war, even losin', we didn't do so bad. I mean it was bad, boys dying, losing they limbs, and eyesight. If'n I had it to do over, I may just wanna think about it this time."

"Why?" Henry said. "That's why they require all the young men to go fight the wars, so as you won't have time to think about it first."

"Lord, all that killin'."

"Now who was it that started that lie about how we in the South was made up all of gentleman, and chivalry, and gave all of us the honorary title of colonel, captain, or judge?"

"Whoever he was, sure as hell had it wrong," John added.

"Yeah," Henry said, "but we bought it, John. We bought into it with both vigor and vitality. All them writers writing them books about the South, paintin' a real purdy picture, but I'm telling you, their ant was ever nothing as bad as it was two maybe three years after we got back to Pickens Co."

"Yeah, they all called it reconstruction."

"Ya know, we can't live in the past," John said.

"Think we need to go to the encampment coming up here in New Orleans," Henry added.

"Ya never know when we gonna be in a position when we ant gonna be able to attend anymore. Besides, we get to reminisce with the boys, and we may get to meet Libby Custer."

"Yeah, well, she was a lot purtier fifty years ago than she is today, by God."

"Yeah, well, who wasn't?" Henry laughed.

"I suppose I'll go. Like ya say, none of us a getting any younger."

"Yeah, well, ya know, the older we be getting, the more special we in they eyes. All the ladies stand up when we walk past," Henry continues.

"Hell, they do that 'cause they all know they safe now. We can't do much at our ages, Henry," John said.

"Well," Henry added, "I still miss my Belinda. We got married soon as I got back, remember?"

"Sure, I remember," John said. "'cause I got married to Maggie Mae pretty soon thereafter, and poor Lil Jake started getting ate up with TB."

"Dadgum, John, you better write that book good as your memory is. Ya know tell the world about our war from a foot soldiers' side of view. Already got more an enough generals telling it from they point of view."

"Ya know, Henry, Maggie Mae and I had eight chilin' learn. Got twenty grandkids and nine great-grandkids."

"Maybe then ya outta write a book on having kids." Henry laughed. "Ya'll had twice as many kids as me and my Belinda.

"See, Belinda was not bashful. Said four kids were enough fer any woman."

"I don't know, John. Women today got so much goin' for them. The world is a changing now. They got the vote and all. Wanna get out and get jobs just like a man. Get to independent nowadays. Hell, they got a female newspaper reporter working out of Atlanta now. Guess they not happy with stayin' home and raising children."

"Well, this is 1925," John replied. "Just think about it, Henry. We lived through our war to see all these changes. Flying machines, motor machines, women voting, Negros with their own newspapers and restaurants. Wonder where it's all gonna end. Ya know we need to go out and shoot that old Spencer I managed to hold on to. 'Cause I think sometimes we may not have made it back here without it."

"I'm thinking all these changes you and me lived through. I wonder what changes our grandbabies and their kids are gonna live to see."

"Well," John replied, "one thing stands out: Everywhere we go, on all the federal and state buildings, you can see the Stars and bars flying.

The Only Death Worth Dying

As eleven- and twelve-year-olds, on Saturday, our favorite playground was the then-deserted army post at Jefferson Barracks back in St. Louis, Missouri. After exploring the deserted buildings and train station and all the empty houses and old cavalry stables, we would discuss the raunchiest girl in class. And as boys, we pondered the question, *Did girls ever fart?* But always before the last bus left the old post, we visited the national cemetery; at that time, nearly all the graves were war related. Remains were yet being returned daily from the battlefields of Europe and the Pacific, also Korea. This was 1953.

Tommy Maloney excitedly waved us over to a large sandstone monument. "Holy shit! You guys, look at this. There are twenty-four names on this one. Guess they went down in a plane crash or something."

The Only Death Worth Dying

Patriotism and vigilance of a newly declared
war in an island paradise so distant from our
sacred home shore, you, in want of heroes, like
we did, endure pain, but for the politician's gain.

Six months of hunger, malaria, and death,
we kept Old Glory flying.

No worry now, for the death of a soldier is
the only death worth dying.

Who is to say if our poetry will ever be written? That's now left to the living for the price of
us indemnifying. Now hear ye my distant voice.

The death of a soldier is the only death worth dying.

We did ponder dreams of grandeur ten thousand sunsets ago; our ghosts are yet riling. The death of a soldier is the only death worth dying, and among broken swords and rusted rifles, they retrieved our bleached white bones and our souls with the albatrosses flying. Hear ye now when I say the death of a soldier is the only death worth dying.

The passage of time now has made our enemies and us all equals, for that day, we also administered to them, the gift they, in turn, gave us—being the death of a soldier is the only death worth dying. Picture us again as you perhaps did then. The sons of whores and working mothers' boys from broken homes, orphanages, and the streets, we now rest humbly with honor under your feet.

History gave to us the greatest destiny. Hold us now without regrets or cries. For the death of a soldier is the only death worth dying.

"Damn, guys. Ya think their families know where they're buried?" Jimmy Coin said.

Tommy Hubbard stood at (Boy Scout) attention and saluted the gravestone. We all at once followed suit.

None of us had a watch, but we knew it was getting late and the last bus was soon to leave Jefferson Barracks, so we hightailed it to the main gate. On the long ride home that day, Jimmy Macready asked me if I had thought anything when we were at that large gravesite.

"The one thing," I answered, "that was the reoccurring thought in my mind was like a voice saying, 'The death of a soldier is the only death worth dying.'"

"Wow!"

Interview with American
Former POW Bataan Survivor

St. Louis, Missouri
Chase Park Plaza hotel, 1982

"Okay, so who was she?" I asked.

"I don't know her name," he answered.

"Only that we heard about her from some Chinese guerillas, operating in the area when we were liberated. Me, like all the rest of the guys, wanted to get home.

"One of the Chinese officers said she was an American agent, posing as a missionary and gathering intelligence on Japanese troop movements and upcoming campaigns, as our relations with the Jap government had recently been severed. Lotta folks said it was the oil embargo. That's when MacArthur put us on full alert in the Philippines.

"They said she decoded the plans for the attack on Pearl Harbor and all the bases in the pacific and North China all the British and Dutch bases were included.

"Of course, I read John Toland's book *Infamy*, and truly it made me angry that every high-level military official in DC knew the exact date and time the attack on Pearl Harbor was to take place, and the only people surprised at the attack were the people at Pearl Harbor.

"She knew. She had something that our government needed to know. But the Japanese had her under surveillance, and finding her radio and endpapers, they executed her on the spot, knowing they would be in a war with us in weeks."

"How come we don't know more about this hero?" I asked.

"Well, I thought it was an interesting story. When I got home, I was going to do some research, but in 1945 on up to today, ya know everything is classified. Maybe the fact she was a woman? Hell, who knows how the government works."

"Maybe she was one of many," I added.

"The idea you ask me about her, whoever she was, or may have been, indicates she is not completely forgotten."

"How about some more Joe?" I motioned for the waiter to refill our cups.

Funny Remembrance

Funny how we remember people, places, and things in our lives and sometimes give credence to the not-so-good memories.

I had breakfast yesterday morning with a friend, and we talked about how our actions bring about results in our lives in proportion to messages we send out to the world by our actions.

The ancients referred to it as the Universal Law, so it's been around for a long time. It all begins with our (my) thinking. My lady friend told me years back (think I mentioned this before), "What we think about, we bring about."

Entertaining healthy thoughts leads to healthy actions of love, acceptance, and forgiveness, and what follows is always an action that leads us up a notch and closer to our highest good. I think it was Buddha who said, "It cannot be otherwise."

Not to say, however, we are all on a personal spiritual quest and are here to grow, learn, and, in many cases, teach either by example or mentoring others who are going through similar struggles related to our personal experiences or our own process of learning.

As most of you all know, I visited the vets the other day to have spirit boy put down, and my interaction with the vet and his techs was quite a life giving. I told him upon leaving, "Thank you, and I love you."

He hugged me and responded. "I love you too."

In today's world, I forget the power of love. It has a healing energy and aura of encompassment that remains beyond words. The very statement of love itself has the power to bring peace to any situation.

The Friendly Goose

Those wonderful sunsets on the water that she and I found, so life giving, sparked many a written word and oil paintings that lifted our spirits, having forsaken the corporate gods and their esurient drive. The wilderness vivified us with unfound energy and diligence. Many winged wonders visited us as we fed all the living things that graced our view as well as our lives. A pair of Canada geese would glide into our yard, often bringing friends and feasting on the hard corn that filled us feeders and troughs.

The seasons came and went. The illness my love had fought for five years finally took her. After the hoopla that goes with a loved one passing, I found myself by the water's edge, the sandstorm in my mind whistling sweet memories. The house was clean and empty. The auctioneer drove the last load away.

The new owners of this paradise would be here in the morning, and I was leaving for Georgia. I felt the emptiness, the hole I knew I would never fill when I saw a lone Canada goose glide down in the yard. She started squawking loudly on the ground, flapping her wings and fussing, angry perhaps that I was leaving?

No, I thought as I locked eyes with this magnificent creature. Hunting season had arrived, and she, like me, was alone.

"You, you lost your mate. You're telling me you're alone too! Or you asking me to fix it? I am sorry for you, my friend. I feel your pain, but life is fleeting—ever fleeting. But then I am told so too is pain."

As she soared off, flying south, I thought of Ginny and the many times we talked of that magical time now lost to the ages when animals and people spoke the same language before the great separation. I yelled at the great goose. "Be safe, my friend. I, too, am going south."

I slumped beneath a big oak tree, knowing, at long last, it was safe to cry.

The Human Makeup

What is the price we pay for ignoring our integrity? Some have a unique way of justifying their actions or behavior. We come with personality. Fear says, "There will never be enough." Somewhere down this road of life, we discover that all our fears were illusions, to begin with.

Say a person can get ahead financially by ripping the other person off and justifying it by saying it was better for everyone in the long run, when in fact it made one a thief and delivered pain to the other.

The lack of integrity is the sacrifice. It will, in time, scar the spirit and fill the mind with distrust as everything you see in the other person is only a mirrored reflection of yourself. Viewing others with suspicion is only viewing your own true self.

Sometimes, our illusions tell us we will only find security if we connive our way into what we think is safety. Enough water, food, guns, other people to control, power, manipulation, sex, money—all of these give the illusion of safety for the insecure. It has only been of late that our own eyes have witnessed what truly happens to the greedy from the Wall Street brokers to the CEOs of enormous corporations.

When we make a conscious decision to do *the next right thing*, and many of us must make this change in our personality at depth, starting out with little actions of fairness and changing old behavior, we intuitively see a difference in our everyday living that gets better with each passing day.

Doing this, we realize we have let go of a great deal of defects and emotional baggage, and a new sense of being and freedom has taken its place. Put this practice in place for thirty days. Sprinkle it with prayerful affirmations and act to change the way you feel about whatever it is that you may want to improve.

Life's Lessons

I learned awhile back in my hometown in St. Louis that other folk's opinions of anything were pretty much just that—an opinion.

Recalling an incident once while I was blaring out my opinion of certain people, places, and things, all of what I thought was "I think this about that and that about this."

A wise lady paused with her coffee and asked me simply, "What's your experience with the people, places, and things you're telling us about?"

I was like, "Pardon me, ma'am, what did you say? My experience? Well, I never really had, ya know, like knowing them?"

"So what your opinion is based on is what others have told you? So you have absolutely no clue if you're even telling us the truth? Sir, that's what is called gossip."

The room fell silent, as did I.

Before I engage anyone today verbally on any topic, I review any personal experience I may have encountered with that person, place, or thing.

For true life experience is difficult to dispute. Today, I learned that sharing anything other than my own experience with the world is nothing less than gossip on a higher scale.

Sharing life's experience gives strength and hope when it benefits others; hence, it becomes an inspiration, at least that's my experience

Remember love. She takes us far.

Come You Back

Come you back age of innocence
Come you back time of my ancestors.
Come you back song of my youth,
When carousel ponies danced me
To sleep.

Might I play this cord from hill tops
We played on and visions we dreamed
In a time, we believed would never
Change.

What did we find in the calmness
Of the sea perhaps the coming of
The autumn breeze times 43 and
The gentle embrace of Jehovah.

Come you back wisdom of Abraham
And come you back in dream and
Song fills you this emptiness and void
Of longing as a father for his child.

Greetings to All My Sisters and Bros

In my experience, I have discovered that life is way too short to carry grudges and spend my (our) days with unforgiving attitudes toward a person, place, or thing.

A continuous practice of gratitude in my life is certainly the best antidote I have found to keep me focused in my day-to-day living. Even knowing occasionally difficult people will show up who I find a challenge in my serenity.

If I am in touch with universal love and practicing some simple, common everyday practices you know, there's no magic over the edge-deep metaphysical word—just the acceptance, love, and tolerance that I need at that given moment.

I will walk away from that situation a better person and have a much better day as a result of honoring that person for him/her being just where he/she is at that given time in life.

Do I fall short? You bet I do, but I don't quit. I do not quit or give up on what I know works.

Acceptance, love, and tolerance of others (a friend once told me this should be my code; she was correct) are the absolute keys to many doors that continue to open in our lives.

Namaste!

Cave Dweller

Oh my, then, what is the answer to this journey with its twists and turns and ups and downs? Its lessons of loss and gain and loss again, scathing relationships that leave one worn and emotionally torn.

The fears that come like tsunamis while the greatest terror remains always with the coming of tomorrow. From womb to cradle, to pompous priest's churchmen and nuns, running naked through a vortex of voices, never looking back.

Where might the wise man be, the holy man or woman who might guide me through this never-ending, ever-increasing tourbillion of confusion and bedlam.

"Struggle," she says, "though you may. One may have life but not without conflict."

Faith Overcomes Fear

The wind blew hard and cold that night as I made my rounds in the prison yard, inspecting the outside doors and entry levels.

Missouri winters are, at times, merciless and unforgiving. I had taken a job with the Missouri Department of Corrections because of having to have medical insurance for my late wife.

From where we lived, the drive to Jefferson City was an hour and a half one way, and I was working the three-eleven shift. It felt, at the time, like trying to make the best of an otherwise not-so-pleasant situation.

I had heard stories of hauntings, sightings, and otherworldly visits from veteran Corrections Officers, but until I experienced it myself, I just brushed it all off.

Of course, some stories I had heard were from the top-ranking officers and staff even then I placed little credence in such converse. Until one night, I was in the basement of house number 2 alone. I thought, *This is a bit creepy.*

I had heard the history of this house that decades before, men had been murdered, raped, and beaten in the basement here where I now stood.

I felt a strong presence beside me. My skin popped with goose bumps. The hair on the back of my neck rose. Turning around in a quick fashion and hand on my Mace can, I saw nothing, but I began to feel encompassed by an invisible presence.

I ran up the steps and, at once, asked the officer upstairs if he was just downstairs.

"No," he replied, "I guess you experienced *the ghost.*"

"*The ghost?*"

"Should have seen Captain Franklyn come runnin' up them steps one night, like to broke his foot getting away from that ghost or whatever it was."

House number 2 was notorious for reported paranormal activities, and many officers and staff refused to work night shift in the huge, old gothic stone structure. It was indeed something right out of an Edgar Allan Poe story.

A nervous newly hired officer, who I worked with on orientation day, came crying to me saying the captain assigned her to housing unit 2 as the officer who was normally staffed there decided it was way too freaky for him and left.

She was frightened of demons or ghosts or whoever may be inhabiting the premises.

I told her to calm down take my hands, and we prayed. I told her to affirm. "There was only one power and one presence at work in her life—God. The all-good, all-present, and the only power—the name of *Jesus Christ* was an absolute truth. No otherworldly entity could stand in the way."

Visions and dreams fill the gap of an unnamed fear and alter from darkness to light my vision whose pinions shield the poison arrows that my enemies hurl upon me.

I stand upon the rock of a promised salvation. The waves below me crash against the rocks as the storm deepens.

I raise my arms in humble thankfulness. Do I not sense the presence of Abraham, Moses, and David?

Might then I praise this day and each new day to the glory of *God of my Fathers*. Do I not sing of thee of what this humble mind might muster?

For it was I who walked through anguish and death. It was thee who delivered me. Let my only prayer be where would thou have me serve thee and with whom and where.

Is Stillness the Mother of Peace?

In quietness, the mind is relieved of the stream of thoughts. I have learned over the years thoughts are ongoing. They have a tendency to derail the wisdom of listening and beg the question, "Do I hear? Or do I interpret?"

I believe, at times, correction from my thoughts and replacing them with awareness are the first steps in undoing age-old belief systems that promote the untruth that separation is a part of our heritage. There is a lesson in A Course in Miracles that begins with "My thoughts do not mean anything." Another lesson says, "My meaningless thoughts are showing me a meaningless world."

Am I not seeing the world through my thoughts? Do I speak from an unfulfilled mind? I read once where Jesus gave only truth, but only eleven got it. His intentions and promises like "You can do what I have done and more" still go unheeded.

Of course, God did not create a meaningless world. It does imply that through my own perception, opinions, and judgments do I view a meaningless world. I believe we do inherit the grace of God. Truth and awareness in my experience come from the stillness, and I have asked myself, Why do I think I need an opinion? I do not.

Through God's mind do I walk toward wholeness and completeness as well as being free from illusion and littleness and the awaking of a deeper knowing of love. Friends warn us about our own thinking. Our friends tell us, "These are thoughts which must go through us constantly. Thy will, not mine, be done—How can I best serve thee?"

How many times have I heard "My mind is not my friend"?

Our minds may be geared toward Hinduism, Islamism, or Christianism. Our thoughts are not real. The only real thought is the thought of God—well, that is profound. Then it occurs to me in truth how we have gotten so caught up in our world with opinions, judgments, and thinking.

Can I pursue God's mind with intensity? Attain the atonement? Embrace God's promise of salvation?

"All things are lessons God would have me learned." A wise person once quoted to me.

CPSIA information can be obtained
at www.ICGtesting.com
Printed in the USA
LVHW020420170322
713568LV00007B/648